To His Son

To His Son

T. Crunk

GreencupBooks

copyright © T. Crunk, 2016

All rights reserved. No part of this manuscript may be copied and distributed except for excerpts for purposes of this book's promotion or for educational purposes.

Printed in the United States

ISBN: 978-1-943661-05-3

GreencupBooks
PO Box 4945
Chattanooga, TN 37405
www.greencupbooks.com

"Daybreak" first appears in issue 2 of *4ink7*.

Cover image: "This Star Teaches Bending," 1940, by Paul Klee

—for Luca

Daybreak   1

To His Son   7

Joyland   45

Daybreak

Comes the last
hour of night
as we sleep—

blue moon
sails back into her harbor
of white clouds

fireflies
night watchmen
snuff their lamps
make their way home

the snails
steadfast guardians
lay down their armor
and rest from their patrol.

Then
first light—

crickets
rise in chorus
strum harps and zithers
a morning
hymn to the sun.

Beetles
emerge from their grottoes
in dark cowls
reciting morning prayers.

At the edge of the harvest field
grasshoppers
sharpen their scythes
waiting
for the white
mist to lift.

Beneath pavilions
of gilded leaves
caterpillars
weave and spin
their regal tapestries

and butterflies
unfold their rich
embroidered robes.

Great caravans
of black ants
embark on expeditions
to undiscovered worlds.

Brigades
of goldclad wasps
return to building
their holy cities
raising high
its parchment temples

and spiders
hoist their fretwork bridges
vaulting
spire to spire.

Troupes
of gypsy gnats
rehearse their aerial ballet.

Dragonflies
in winged chariots
set out across the pond

as legions of locusts
din from the bank—
Pha-raoh
Pha-raoh
Pha-raoh

and retinues
of water striders
perform their daily miracle.

Then
we wake

to daybreak

the world beginning

rise
as morning rises

greet the dawning
as it passes

grateful

for this day
of small things.

To His Son

Shadow and light
dawn and night

Water and earth
time and birth

The beginning
begins
its beginning
around go
round around

What then
shall we make
a world of?
and what shall we
make of it now?

First
the beasts

of the field
and fowl

of the air
your elders—

each is liege
in her own

sacred dominion
theirs

are the gods
of splendor

and of miracle

of worlds
and of riches

unimaginable
to you

who must
learn their ways

and be humble

                                    Leaf and tree
                                    hive and bee

                                    Rose and thorn
                                    barley and corn

                                    Murrey apple
                                    tawny pear
                                    dogwood blossoms
                                    for your hair

                                    Leagrass rest you
                                    birch bough bless you

                    Nursling
                    of the greensward fair

And the plants
of the field

green grace
of the earth

these
are your body—

morning glories
opening

are your eyes
to the day

redbud blooming
your sweet blood

in its coursing

sycamore and hackberry
great bones

that stand you

bamboo
sifting a breeze

your call
to sleep—

they are
your living

so your duty
and your joy:

attend
attend

                      Whistle and hum
                      fiddle and strum

                      Stick and ball
                      wagon and doll

                      Sound the horn
                      clang the bell
                      sing the rhyme
                      chant the spell

                      Raise the flag
                      bang the drum
                      start the game
                      chase the sun

Then music!

banjo rain

your tam
-bourine heart

drum of water
falling seaward

soft flute
of your breathing

oboe rising
life into sapbranch

tendril and vine

your penny
-whistle voice.

Then the going
and the finding!

dirt
is for digging

(this world
is earth

and the ancients
we discover there)

stones
are a hard knock

bones in a puddle
can on a fence

the sky is flying

cloudscarf and flag
rags in the wind

—so much so big
and you

so small

so new so old
and you

becoming time

O ride
then ride

the forever
of now

O ride
no stopping

angelwise

bicycle

to the sun!

                                      Kith and kin
                                      help and friend

                                      Book and globe
                                      map and scroll

                                      Hand to hand
                                      the circle joining
                                      hand to hand
                                      the dance rejoicing

                                      Heart to heart
                                      in love abound
                                      turn and turn
                                      a world comes round

Yes
the world is

big and
you are small

but you
will grow bigger

you will need

other hands

other minds

first
mother father

hand hand hand

now
you are three

big as a home

then aunts and uncles
cousins all

now you are many
more and more

then friend and neighbor
teacher and friend

and stranger too
and all you meet

the circle turning
far and wide

and so it grows
big as a world.

And other minds

you will need
their books:

The Book of Light
its showing forth

its shining
in all things

The Book of Long Ago
of how

what was
became

and is becoming
what it is

Book of Laughter
Book of Healing

The Book of Stories
worlds created

from the All-
And-Nothing

that is words

The Book of Questing

of how we near

the far away
the everfar

Book of Wonders
Book of Signs & Numbers

The Book of Sorrows too

our fallings
and our failings

lost cities
lost lives

father mother child

trailing dust
along a parched road

seeking
some new home

Book of Wheels
of endless turnings

Book of Earth and Sky
mazes and lightning

The Book of Art

of what can be

which also
is The Book of Joy

The Book of Wisdom
of what should be

which also
is The Book of Justice—

so you grow
the circle joining

hand to hand
heart to mind

large and rich
as any world

the world
that will be you.

                        Sign and symbol
                        rune and riddle

                        Clue and cipher
                        hint and whisper

                        What do you see?
                        dust in the sun
                        what do you hear?

a voice in the wind

What could it be?
it has no name
something or nothing?
all the same

Know too
there is

another world

as you walk about
be heedful:

each found coin

or ticket stub
on the sidewalk

each playing card
in the gutter

(six
of hearts—?)

is a sign
a revelation

no reading them
no vexing

with interpretation

it is enough
to know

they are tokens
glyphs

from that
other world

and that world
is

in this one

                                        Road and rail
                                        ship and sail

                                        Track and train
                                        bus and plane

                                        How far
                                        does this road go
                                        my friend?

                                        How far
                                        does this road go?

All the way
to the end
my friend

All the way
to the end

And then
the time of leaving

your traveler's grip
on the platform

mother father
waiting with you—

so know this now
about journeys:

you may not see
where leaving leads

but be sure
that any road

holds its blessing

any land
its promise

(though beware

the one that

any god
calls you to)

and you may find

not
what you seek

but what you
need to find

which may lie

in joys
yet undiscovered

but may
lie hidden too

in what you fear
or hurts you

(such are journeys)

lastly
not all goings

take you
simply here to there

some are wayward

ranging out
spiraling in

turning
and returning

but this too
if it awaits

is
as it should be

as journeys
take us

not
vice-versa

be assured then
time itself

will see
to your arriving

—but there
the whistle

calls you now
down the bend

one of hearts

our love with you
in going

to take
some new place

in our lives
and in your own

                    Course and path
                    lamp and staff

                    Church and school
                    writ and rule

                    And when the devil
                    stops his wagon
                    at your gate
                    at your gate

                    Looking for
                    a soul to take

                    Say—
                    move along
                    Old Grizzlebeard
                    Old Grizzlebeard

                    There's nothing

for you here

As for commandments
they are few—

    love your life
    and be grateful

    live with grace
    and be kind

—and they are
all the same

    Ax and spade
    tool and trade

    Shop and mill
    forge and kiln

    Clock and time
    dollar and dime

    Hand to wheel
    back to plow
    pull of sinew
    sweat of brow

    When work is done
    then all may rest
    if work be goodly

all are blessed

As for work:

if you
will be a sailor

sail every sea

if you will
be a weaver

run every thread
taut and true

if a man of books

read deeply
teach wisely

if a potter
bring the earth

to life
in your two hands

a life
to pass along

but know
the man who

builds your house
may sleep

without a roof
the mother

harvesting your food
may hunger

the child
who sews your coat

may go without
and rue the cold—

be fruitful then
and joyful

in your work
but O

dear
god of mercy:

attend
attend

                                      Mother bed
                                      Father coffin

Mother bed
Father coffin

Dark the day
and darker night
grief bereaves
the world of light

Deathcrow strutting
in his blacks
calls you
down a godlorn path

There will
be wilderness years

you will find
you are lost

you will see
you are entering

a dark wood

then enter it
as it enters you

black rays

fingering down
through the trees

no beast
stalking you

but a faint
flutter of wing

unseen
in a high nest

no other sound

but the
low keening

of the silence
you bear

and have become

you will not know
which way

is forward
for there is no way

time has died

and with it
all movement

all passing

all passing through

you may
turn and turn

you may at times
lie still

longing
for an end

or ending

and yes
it will at last

be done

likely
against
your own doing

and somehow
implausibly

you will
step out

beneath a
clear nightsky

drained of darkness

waning
into dawn

dusted
with morning stars

that have
always been there

each one
a prayer

that we
have prayed

in our own darkness

mercy
for your safekeeping

                                          Stitch and sew
                                          plant and grow

                                          One and one
                                          a life begun

                                          Hand to hand
                                          the circle joining
                                          hand to hand

the dance rejoicing

Heart to heart
in love abound
turn and turn
a world comes round

Then
you will find

that love
and only love

can redeem

this sorrow
-haunted life

without love
all is nothing

but with love
anything is all

and the sacredness
of all

with love
your hand's reaching

may finally end

and breath
will be a touching

not a gathering
and releasing

of absence

with love
night is not

an enduring

time is not
a falling away

but an increase
(one day less

in fact
is one day more)

without love

going
is only wandering

but with love
there is no going

only being

here

then here
then here—

        a path
        along a river

        a stony point
        among blue hills

        low wall
        by a summer meadow

        house
        being built

        garden
        being planted

        a home

        in this
        fell world

        life
        being living

                Hammer and nail
                ladder and pail

Brick and stone
hearth and home

Grandmother lamp
Grandfather clock
Uncle chair
Aunt cooking pot

Three good wishes
mother father
three good kisses
at the altar

Build your house now
build it strong
time is coming
here and gone

Then the time
of building

your life
grown so rich

in blessings
and in sorrows

gifts
and losses too

you cannot
contain it

so lay brick
hoist beams
true doors

a house for joy
and joy's children

but know that
building is

but a brief
togethering

against
the goings away

for as you build
time unbuilds

the world
of your father

vanishing
even now

long lost
the world

of your
father's father

they too

built earnestly
as you

but all
that remains

are these
few stories—

here this cup
this clock

here this lamp
this photograph

—so beware possessions

as most
are dead matter

but fill your house
with remnants

alive with stories

of the going
and the gone

they are all
that will endure

all that
will abide

for joy
and joy's children

                                        Smoke and rain
                                        link and chain

                                        Ash and coal
                                        heart and soul

                                        The beginning
                                        begins
                                        its beginning
                                        around go
                                        round around

                                        What then
                                        will you make
                                        a new world of?
                                        and what will you
                                        make of it now?

And so in time
you will

come to this—
your children

starting
lives anew

their own
and yours

and you
will need for

strength
to strengthen them

counsel
to guide them

in their passage

but at the last
I have

no wisdom for you

(you must
find your own)

just a prayer—

that you
and they

may find rest
beside the cool

easy waters
and flourish

in the shade of
the spreading

godtree
its sheltering arms

with joy of soul
heart of love
mind at peace

but knowing
too:

this is
your only life

and this world
will never

never
be enough

Shadow and light
dawn and night

Body and breath
time and death

High on a hill
where shadows fly
your bones will sleep
by and by

By and by

Down in a valley
where the bloodthorn grows
ghosts sing a song
that nobody knows

Nobody knows

And when your father
sheds this life

to begin
his sojourn

in that
Night Country

he will
take his place

among all

that is There-
But-Not-There

the wonder of it

that you
have ever known:

dust
in a ray of sun

puzzles of light

wind
in the leaves

music

cricketsong
in the closing darkness

moon

a shadow
whispering

a dream

Joyland

We can see the lights
of Joyland
from our bedroom window.

At night
we lie awake
and dream of it.

Joyland
is on the other side of the river
that runs behind our house

the lights like stars
like constellations
come swirling down to earth.

The gates of Joyland
rise up—

red and golden columns
pink angels flying across the top

... JOYLAND ...
spelled out in blue lights
across their white robes
flowing out behind them.

When you pass through the gates
a guard in a scarlet uniform
takes your ticket

gives you balloons
floating like clouds on silk cords
and says—Welcome!
Welcome to Joyland!

You have always dreamed
of being here
and now that you are
you are not sure what to do first.

So you set out
on the bright path
shining before you....

Under a painted tent
the Juggler
balances on his tightrope
tosses rainbow-colored scarves over his head
up and up.

They turn into white doves
and fly away.

The Fire Eater
in his gypsy turban
licks a tongue of flame from his hand
blows it out again—

a yellow rose of fire
blooming
into the air above him.

In her fortune teller's booth
Madame Sosostris
spins the number wheel.

If it stops on 7
you will have a safe journey.
If it stops on 3
you will find what you are seeking.

The Weaver
spins out cotton candy
into beautiful shapes.

You may choose an emerald crown
with butterscotch stars.
You may choose an orange torch
sparkling
with cinnamon light.

The carousel animals
sing for you
and tell you stories
as you ride them.

They tell you
where the sun
sleeps in his cave at night.

They tell you
where the ants
sew their tiny wedding dresses.

You tell them
your secrets.

In the House of Mirrors
you have many faces.
Which is yours—
this one? that one?

When you come out again
you have only one—
your own.

At the edge
of the Crystal Lake
you step into
your swan-drawn boat.

The four
Sea Graces appear
to guide you
to the other shore.

Their silver hair
gleams
in the moonlight.

They bring you
finally
to the Ferris wheel
great circle of light.

You have saved this
for last.

You step into
your winged carriage.

It lifts you
up into the blue night

up
toward the yellow moon
nodding above

the cool breeze
brushing your face.

And when you reach the top
you look out
across the river

and there
you see your house.

You look into
your bedroom window

and there
you see yourself

sleeping

your hand curled up
around a small green jewel
on the pillow beside you...

About the Author

T. Crunk's first collection of poetry, *Living in the Resurrection,* was a Yale Series of Younger Poets selection. He is the author of numerous subsequent poetry collections, children's books, and works of fiction.

www.ingramcontent.com/pod-product-compliance
Lightning Source LLC
Chambersburg PA
CBHW021452080526
44588CB00009B/815